Freedom Through Disobedience

Chitta Ranjan Das

Alpha Editions

This edition published in 2022

ISBN : 9789356310445

Design and Setting By
Alpha Editions
www.alphaedis.com
Email - info@alphaedis.com

FREEDOM THROUGH DISOBEDIENCE

The following is the full text of the Presidential Address of Desabhandhu C. R. Das at the thirty-seventh session of the Indian National Congress held at Gaya on 26th December 1922:—

SISTERS AND BROTHERS,—

As I stand before you to-day, a sense of overwhelming loss overtakes me, and I can scarce give expression to what is uppermost in the minds of all and everyone of us. After a memorable battle which he gave to the Bureaucracy, Mahatma Gandhi has been seized and cast into prison; and we shall not have his guidance in the proceedings of the Congress this year. But there is inspiration for all of us in the last stand which he made in the citadel of the enemy, in the last defiance which he hurled at the agents of the Bureaucracy. To read a story equal in pathos, in dignity, and in sublimity you have to go back over two thousand years, when Jesus of Nazareth, "as one that perverted the people" stood to take his trial before a foreign tribunal.

"And Jesus stood before the Governor: and the Governor asked him saying, Art thou the king of the Jews? And Jesus said unto him, Thou sayëst.

"And when he has accused of the chief priests and elders, he answered nothing.

"Then said Pilate unto him, Hearest thou not how many things they witness against thee?

"And he answered him too never a word; insomuch that the Governor marvelled greatly."

Mahatma Gandhi took a different course. He admitted that he was guilty, and he pointed out to the public Prosecutor, that his guilt was greater than he, the Prosecutor, had alleged; but he maintained that if he had offended against the law of Bureaucracy in so offending, he had obeyed the law of God. If I may hazard a guess, the Judge who tried him and who passed a sentence of imprisonment on him was filled with the same feeling of marvel as Pontius Pilate had been.

Great in taking decisions, great in executing them, Mahatma Gandhi was incomparably great in the last stand which he made on behalf of his country. He is undoubtedly one of the greatest men that the world has ever seen. The world hath need of him and if he is mocked and jeered at by "the people of importance," the "people with a stake in the country"—Scribes and Pharisees of the days of Christ he will be gratefully remembered now and always by a nation which he led from victory to victory.

"LAW AND ORDER"

Gentlemen, the time is a critical one and it is important to seize upon the real issue which divides the people from the Bureaucracy and its Indian allies. During the period of repression which began about this time last year, it was this issue which pressed itself on our attention. This policy of repression was supported and in some cases instigated by the Moderate Leaders who are in the Executive Government. I do not charge those who supported the Government with dishonesty or want of patriotism. I say they were led away by the battle cry of Law and Order. And it is because I believe that there is a fundamental confusion of thought behind this attitude of mind that I propose to discuss this plea of Law and Order. "Law and Order" has indeed been the last refuge of Bureaucracies all over the world.

It has been gravely asserted not only by the Bureaucracy but also by its apologists, the Moderate Party, that a settled Government is the first necessity of any people and that the subject has no right to present his grievances except in a constitutional way, by which I understand in some way recognised by the constitution. If you cannot actively co-operate in the maintenance of "the law of the land" they say, "it is your duty as a responsible citizen to obey it passively. Non-resistance is the least that the Government is entitled to expect from you."

This is the whole political philosophy of the Bureaucracy—the maintenance of law and order on the part of the Government, and an attitude of passive obedience and non-resistance on the part of the subject. But was not that the political philosophy of every English King from William the Conqueror to James II? And was not that the political philosophy of the Romanoffs, the Hohenzollerns and of the Bourbons? And yet freedom has come, where it has come, by disobedience of the very laws which were proclaimed in the name of law and order. Where the Government is arbitrary and despotic and the fundamental rights of the people are not recognised, it is idle to talk of law and order.

The doctrine has apparently made its way to this country from England. I shall, therefore, refer to English history to find out the truth about this doctrine. That history has recorded that most of the despots in England who exercised arbitrary sway over the people proposed to act for the good of the people and for the maintenance of law and order. English absolutism from the Normans down to the Stuarts tried to put itself on a constitutional basis through the process of this very law and order. The pathetic speech delivered by Charles I. just before his execution puts the whole doctrine in a nutshell. "For the people," he said, "truly I desire their liberty and freedom as much as anybody whatsoever, but I must tell you that their liberty and freedom consist in having Government, those laws by which their lives and their goods may be their own. It is not their having a share in the Government, that is nothing appertaining to them. A subject and a sovereign are clear different things." The doctrine of law and order could not be stated with more admirable clearness. But though the English kings acted constitutionally in the sense that their acts were in accordance with the letter of law and were covered by precedents, the subjects always claimed that they were free to assert their fundamental rights and to wrest them from the king by force or insurrections. The doctrine of law and order received a rude shock when King John was obliged to put his signature to the Magna Charta on the 15th of June, 1215. The 61st clause of the Charter is important for our purpose securing as it did to the subject the liberty of rebellion as a means for enforcing the due observance of the Charter by the Crown. Adams, a celebrated writer of English Constitutional History, says that the conditional right to rebel is as much at the foundation of the English Constitution to-day as it was in 1215. But though the doctrine of law and order had received a rude shock it did not altogether die; for in the intervening period the Crown claimed and asserted the right to raise money, not only by indirect taxes but also by forced loans and benevolences; and frequently exercised large legislative functions not only by applying what are known as suspending and dispensing powers but also by issuing proclamations. The Crown claimed, as Hallam says, "not only a kind of supplemental right of legislation to perfect and carry out what the spirit of existing laws might require but also a paramount supremacy, called sometimes the king's absolute or sovereign power which sanctioned commands beyond the legal prerogative, for the sake of public safety whenever the Council might judge that to be in hazard." By the time of the Stuarts the powers claimed by the Crown were recognised by the courts of law as well founded, and, to quote the words of Adams, "the forms of law became the engines for the perpetration of judicial murders." It is necessary to remember that it was the process of law and order that helped to consolidate the powers of the Crown; for it was again and again laid down by the Court of Exchequer that the power of taxation was vested in the Crown, where it was "for the general benefit of the people." As Adams says, "the Stuarts asserted a legal justification for everything done by them," and, "on the whole, history was with the king."

But how did the Commons meet this assertion of law and order? They were strict non-co-operators both within and outside the Parliament. Within the Parliament they again and again refused to vote supplies unless their grievances were redressed. The King retorted by raising Customs duties on his own initiative and the courts of law supported him. The Commons passed a resolution to the effect that persons paying them "should be reputed betrayers of the liberties of England and enemies to the same." There was little doubt that revolution was on the land; and King Charles finding himself in difficulty gave his Royal Assent to the Bill of Rights on the 17th of June 1626. The Bill of Rights constitutes a triumph for N. C. O's; for it was by their refusal to have any part or share in the administration of the country that the Commons compelled the King to acknowledge their Rights. The events that followed between 1629 and 1640 made the history of England. In spite of the Bill of Rights the King continued to raise customs duties and Elliot and his friends were put on their trial. They refused to plead and the result was disastrous for the arbitrary power of the King. The King levied ship money on the nation. The chief constables of various places replied that the sherrifs had no authority to assess or tax any man without the consent of the Parliament. On the refusal on the part of the people to pay the taxes, their cattle was destrained and no purchaser could be found for them. The King took the opinion of the Exchequer Court on the question "when the good and the safety of the kingdom is concerned and the whole kingdom is in danger." Mark how the formula has been copied verbatim in the Government of India Act. "May not the king command all the subjects of his kingdom, to provide and furnish such a number of ships with men, victuals and munitions and for such time as he shall think fit for the defence and safeguard of the Kingdom from such peril"—again the formula "and by law compel the doing thereof in case of refusal any refractoriness? And whether in such case is not the King the sole judge, both of the danger and when and how the same is to be prevented?" The Judges answered in the affirmative and maintained the answer in the celebrated case which Hampden brought before them.

I desire to emphasise one point and that is that throughout the long and bitter struggle between the Stuarts and Parliament, the Stuarts acted for the maintenance of Law and Order, and there is no doubt that both law and history were on their side. On the eve of the Civil War, the question that divided the parties was this: could the Crown, in the maintenance of Law and Order, claim the passive obedience of the subject or was there any power of resistance in the subject, though that resistance might result in disorder and in breaches of law? The adherents of the Parliament stood for power and the majesty of the people, the authority and independence of Parliament, individual liberty, the right to resist and the right to compel abdication and deposition of the Crown, in a word, they stood by them against the coercive power of the State. The adherence of the Crown stood for indefeasible rights—a right to claim passive obedience and secure non-resistance on the part of the subject through the process of Law and Order; in a word, they stood for State coercion and compulsory co-operation against individual liability.

The issue was decided in favour of Parliament but as it must happen in every war of arms, the victory for individual liberty was only temporary. Though the result of Civil War was disastrous from the point of view of individual liberty, and though it required another revolution—this time, a non-violent revolution—to put individual liberty on a sure foundation "the knowledge that the subject had sat in rude judgment on their King, man to man, speeded the slow emancipation of the mind from the shackles of custom and ancient reverence."

The Revolution of 1688—a bloodless revolution—secured for England that Rule of Law which is the only sure foundation for the maintenance of Law and Order. It completed the work which the Long Parliament had begun and which the execution of Charles I. had interrupted. But how was the peaceful revolution of 1688 brought about? By defiance of authority and by rigid adherence to the principle that it is the inalienable right of the subject to resist the exercise by the executive of wide, arbitrary or discretionary powers of constraint.

The principle for which the revolution of 1688 stood was triumphantly vindicated in the celebrated case of Dr. Sacheverell. In the course of a sermon which he had preached, he gave expression to the following sentiment. "The grand security of our Government and the very pillar upon which it stands is founded upon the steady belief of the subjects' obligation to an absolute and unconditional obedience to the supreme power in all things lawful and the utter illegality of resistance on any pretence whatsoever." This is the doctrine of passive obedience and non-resistance the doctrine of law and order, which is proclaimed to-day by every bureaucrat in the country, foreign or domestic and which is supposed to be the last word on the subjects' duty and Government's rights. But mark how they solved the problem in England in 1710. The Commons impeached Dr. Sacheverell giving expression to a view so destructive of individual liberty and the Lords by a majority of votes found him guilty. The speeches delivered in the course of the trial are interesting. I desire to quote a few sentences from some of those speeches. Sir Joseph Jekyll in the course of his speech said, "that as the Law is the only measure of the Princes' authority and the peoples' subjection, so the law derives its being and efficacy from common consent; and to place it on any other foundation than common consent is to take away the obligation." This notion of common consent puts both prince and people under, to observe the laws.

"My Lords, as the doctrine of unlimited non-resistance was impliedly renounced by the whole nation in the resolution, so diverse Acts of Parliament afterwards passed expressing their renunciation, ... and, therefore I shall only say that it can never be supposed that the laws were made to set up a despotic power to destroy themselves and to warrant subversion of a constitution of a Government which they were designed to establish and defend." Mr. Walpole put the whole argument in a nutshell when he said, "the doctrine of unlimited, unconditional passive obedience was first invented to support arbitrary and despotic power and was never promoted or countenanced by any Government that had not designs sometime or other of making use of it." The argument against the doctrine of Law and Order could not be put more clearly or forcibly, for his argument comes to this: "that the doctrine is not an honest one if law and order is the process by which absolution consolidates its powers and strengthens its hand." I will make one more quotation and that is from the speech of Major-Gen. Stanhope. "As to the doctrine itself of absolute non-resistance, it should seem needless to prove by argument that it is inconsistent with the law of reason, with the law of Nature and with the practice of all ages and countries.... And indeed one may appeal to the practice of all Churches and of all states and of all nations in the world, how they behaved themselves when they found their civil and religious constitutions invaded and oppressed by tyranny."

This then is the history of the freedom movement in England. The conclusion is irresistible that it is not by acquiescence in the doctrine of Law and Order that the English people have obtained the recognition of their fundamental rights. It follows from the survey that I have made firstly that no regulation is law unless it is based on the consent of the people; secondly where such consent is wanting the people are under no obligation to obey; thirdly, where such laws are not only not based on the consent of the people but profess to attack their fundamental rights the subjects are entitled to compel their withdrawal by force or insurrections; fourthly, that Law and Order is and has always been a plea for absolutism and lastly there can be neither law nor order before the real reign of Law begins.

I have dealt with the question at some length as the question is a vital one and there are many Moderates who still think that it is the duty of every loyal subject to assist the Government in the maintenance of Law and Order. The personal liberty of every Indian to-day depends to a great extent on the exercise by persons in authority of wide, arbitrary or discretionary powers. Where such powers are allowed the rule of law is denied. To find out the extent to which this exploded doctrine of Law and Order influences the minds of sober and learned men we have only to read the report of the Committee appointed to examine the repressive laws. You will find in the report neither the vision of the patriot nor the wisdom of the statesman; but you will find an excessive worship of that much advertised but much misunderstood phrase "Law and Order." "Why is Regulation III of 1818 to be amended and kept on the Statute Book?" Because for the protection of the frontiers of India and the fulfilment of the responsibility of the Government of India in relation to Indian States there must be some enactment to arm the executive with powers to restrict the movements and activities of certain persons, who though not coming within the scope of any criminal law have to be put under some measure of restraint. Why are the Indian Criminal Law Amendment Act 1908 and the Prevention of Seditious Meetings Act 1911 to be retained on the Statute Book? For the preservation of law and order? They little think these learned gentlemen responsible for the report that these Statutes, giving as they do to the Executive wide, arbitrary and discretionary powers of constraint, constitute a state of things wherein it is the duty of every individual to resist and to defy the tyranny of such lawless laws. These Statutes in themselves constitute a breach of law and order, for, law and order is the result of the rule of law; and where you deny the existence of the rule of law, you cannot turn round and say it is your duty as law-abiding citizens to obey the law.

We have had abundance of this law and order during the last few years of our National History. The last affront delivered to the nation, was the promulgation of an executive order under the authority of the Criminal Law Amendment Act making the legitimate work of Congress Volunteers illegal and criminal. This was supported by our Moderate friends on the ground that it is the duty of the law-abiding subject to support the maintenance of law and order. The doctrine, as I said before, has travelled all the way from the shores of England. But may I ask—is there one argument advanced to-day by the Bureaucracy and its friends which was not advanced with equal clearness by the Stuarts? When the Stuarts arrogated to themselves a discretionary power of committing to prison all persons who were on any account obnoxious to the Court, they made the excuse that the power was necessary for the safety of the nation. And the power was resisted in England, not because it was never exercised for the safety of the nation, but because the existence of the power was inconsistent with the existence, at the same time of individual liberty. When the Stuarts claimed the right to legislate by proclamation and by the wide exercise of suspending and dispensing powers they did so on the express ground that such legislation was necessary for public safety. That right was denied by the English nation, not because such legislation was not necessary for public safety but because such right could not co-exist with the fundamental right of the nation to legislate for itself. Is the power of the Governor-General to certify that the passage of a Bill is essential for safety or tranquility or interest of British India, any different from the power claimed by the Stuarts? There is indeed a striking resemblance between the power conferred on the Governor-General and the Governors of the provinces and the powers claimed by the Tudors and the Stuarts. When the Stuarts claimed the right to raise revenue on their own initiative, they disclaimed any intention to exercise such right except "when the good and safety of the kingdom in general is concerned and the whole kingdom is in danger." That right was resisted in England, not because the revenues raised by them were not necessary for the good and safety of the kingdom, but because that right was inconsistent with the fundamental right of the people to pay such taxes only as were determined by the representatives of the people for the people. Is the power conferred on the Governor to certify that the expenditure provided for by a particular demand not assented to by the legislature is essential to the discharge of his responsibility for the subjects, any different from the power claimed by the Stuarts? It should be patent to everybody that we do not live under any history of England as proclaimed that it is idle to talk of the maintenance of law and order when large discretionary powers of constraint are vested in the executive. The manhood of England triumphantly resisted the pretensions of "Law and Order." If there is manhood in India to-day, India will successfully resist the same pretensions, advanced by the Indian Bureaucracy.

I have quoted from English History at length, because the argument furnished by that history appeals to people who are frightened by popular movement into raising the cry of "law and order." Follow the lines laid down in that History. For myself, I oppose the pretensions of "law and order" not on historical precedent, but on the ground that it is the inalienable right of every individual and of every nation to stand on truth and to offer a stubborn resistance to the promulgation of lawless laws. There was a law in the time of Christ which forbade the people from eating on the Sabbath, but allowed the priests to profane Sabbath. And how Christs dealt with the law is narrated in the New Testament.

"At that time Jesus went on the Sabbath day through the corn; and his disciples were an hungered, and began to pluck the ear of corn and to eat.

"But when the Pharisses saw it, they said unto him, Behold, thy disciples do that which is not lawful to do upon the Sabbath day.

"But he said unto them, have we not read what David did, when he was an hungered and they that were with him;

"How he entered into the House of God and did eat the shew bread, which was not lawful for him to eat, neither for them which were with him, but only for the priests?

"Or have we not read in the law, how that on the Sabbath days the priests in the temple profaned the Sabbath and are blameless?"

The truth is that law and order is for man, and not man for law and order. The development of nationality is a sacred task and anything which impedes that task is an obstacle which the very force and power of nationality must overcome. If therefore you interpose a doctrine to impede the task why, the doctrine must go. If you have recourse to law and order to establish and defend the rule of law, then your law and order is entitled to claim the respect of all law-abiding citizens, but, as soon as you have recourse to it not to establish and defend the rule of law, but to destroy and attack it, there is no longer any obligation on us to respect it, for a Higher Law, the virtual law, the Law of God compels to offer our stubborn resistance to it. When I find something put forward in the sacred name of law and order that it is deliberately intended to hinder the growth, the development, and the self-realization of the nation, I have no hesitation whatever in proclaiming that such law and order is an outrage on man and an insult to God.

But though our Moderate friends are often deluded by the battle cry of law and order, I rejoice when I hear that cry. It means that the Bureaucracy is in danger and that the Bureaucracy has realised its danger. It is not without reason that the false issue is raised and the fact a false issue has been raised fills me with hope and courage. I ask my countrymen to be patient and to press the charge. Freedom has already advanced when the alarm of law and order is sounded; that is the history of Bureaucracies all over the world.

In the meantime it is our duty to keep our ideal steadfast. We must not forget that we are on the eve of great changes, that world forces are working all around us and that the battle of freedom has yet to be won.

NATIONALISM: THE IDEAL

What is the ideal which we must set before us? The first and foremost is the ideal of nationalism. Now what is Nationalism? It is, I conceive, a process through which a nation expresses itself and finds itself, not in isolation from other nations but, as part of a great scheme by which, in seeking its own expression and therefore its own identity, it materially assists the self-expression and self-realization of other nations as well. Diversity is as real as Unity. And in order that the unity of the world may be established it is essential that each nationality should proceed on its own lines and find fulfilment in self-expression and self-realisation. The Nationality of which I am speaking must not be confused with the conception of nationality as it exists in Europe to-day. Nationalism in Europe is an aggressive nationalism, a selfish nationalism, a commercial nationalism of gain and loss. The gain of France is a loss of Germany, and the gain of Germany is a loss of France. Therefore French nationalism is nurtured on the hatred of Germany and German nationalism is nurtured in the hatred of France. It is not yet realised that you cannot hurt Germany without hurting Humanity and in consequence hurting France; and that you cannot hurt France without hurting Humanity, and in consequence hurting Germany. That is European nationalism; that is not the nationalism of which I am speaking to you to-day. I contend that each nationality constitutes a particular stream of the great unity, but no nation can fulfil itself until it becomes itself and at the same time realises its identity with Humanity. The whole problem of nationalism is therefore to find that stream and to face the destiny. If you find the current and establish a continuity with the past, then the process of self-expression has begun, and nothing can stop the growth of nationality.

Throughout the pages of Indian history, I find a great purpose unfolding itself. Movement after movement has swept over this vast country, apparently creating hostile forces, but in reality stimulating the vitality and moulding the life of the people into one great nationality. If the Aryans and the non-Aryans met, it was for the purpose of making one people out of them. Brahmanism with its great culture succeeded in binding the whole of India and was indeed a mighty unifying force. Buddhism with its protests against Brahmanism served the same great historical purposes and from Magadha to Taxila was one great Buddhistic empire which succeeded not only in broadening the basis of Indian unity, but in creating what is perhaps more important, the greater India beyond the Himalayas and beyond the seas, so much so that the sacred city where we have met may be regarded as a place of pilgrimage of millions and millions of people of Asiatic races. Then came the Mahomedans of divers races, but with one culture which was their common heritage. For a time it looked as if there was a disintegrating force, an enemy to the growth of Indian nationalism, but the Mahomedans made their home in India, and, while they brought a new outlook and a wonderful vitality to the Indian life, with infinite wisdom, they did as little as possible to disturb the growth of life in the villages where India really lives. This new outlook was necessary for India: and if the two sister streams met, it was only to fulfil themselves and face the destiny of Indian history. Then came the English with their alien culture, their foreign methods, delivering a rude shock to this growing nationality; but the shock has only completed the unifying process so that the purpose of history is practically fulfilled. The great Indian nationality is in sight. It already stretches its hands across the Himalayas not only to Asia but to the whole of the world, not aggressively, but to demand its recognition, and to offer its contribution, I desire to emphasise that there is no hostility between the ideal of nationality and that of world-peace. Nationalism is the process through which alone will world-peace come. A full and unfettered growth of nationalism is necessary for world-peace just as a full and unfettered growth of individuals is necessary for nationality. It is the conception of aggressive nationality in Europe that stands in the way of peace; but once the truth is grasped that it is not possible for a nation to inflict a loss on another nation without at the same time inflicting a loss on itself, the problem of Humanity is solved. The essential truth of nationality lies in this, that it is necessary for each nation to develop itself, express itself and realise itself, so that Humanity itself may develop itself, express itself and realise itself. It is my belief that this truth of nationality will endure, although, for the moment, unmindful of the real issue, the nations are fighting amongst themselves and, if I am not mistaken, it is the very instinct of selfishness and self-preservation which will ultimately solve the problem, not the narrow and the mistaken selfishness of the present, but a selfishness universalized by intellect and transfigured by spirit, a selfishness that will bring home to the nations of the world that in the efforts to put down their neighbours lies their own ruin and suppression.

We have, therefore, to foster the spirit of Nationality. True development of the Indian nation must necessarily lie in the path of Swaraj. A question has often been asked as to what is Swaraj. Swaraj is indefinable and is not to be confused with any particular system of Government. There is also the difference in the world between Swarajya and Samrajya. Swaraj is the natural expression of the national mind. The full outward expression of that mind covers, and must necessarily cover, the whole life history of a nation. Yet it is true that Swaraj begins when the true development of a nation begins, because, as I have said, Swaraj is the expression of the national mind.

The question of nationalism, therefore, looked at from another point of view, is the same question as that of Swaraj. The question of all questions in India to-day is the attainment of Swaraj.

NON-VIOLENT NON-CO-OPERATION

I now come to the question of method. I have to repeat that it has been proved beyond any doubt that the method of non-violent non-co-operation is the only method which we must follow to secure a system of Government which may in reality be the foundation of Swaraj. It is hardly necessary to discuss the philosophy of non-co-operation. I shall simply state the different view-points from which this question may be discussed.

From the national point of view the method of non-co-operation means the attempt of the nation to concentrate upon its own energy and to stand on its own strength. From the ethical point of view, non-co-operation means the method of self-purification, the withdrawal from that which is injurious to the development of the nation, and therefore to the good of humanity. From the spiritual point of view Swaraj means that isolation which in the language of Sadhana is called protyahar—that withdrawal from the forces which are foreign to our nature—an isolation and withdrawal which is necessary in order to bring out from our hidden depths the soul of the nation in all her glory. I do not desire to labour the point, but from every conceivable point of view, the method of non-violent non-co-operation must be regarded as the true method of "following in the path of Swaraj."

FORCE AND VIOLENCE

Doubt has, however, been expressed in some quarters about the soundness of the principle of non-violence. I cannot refuse to acknowledge that there is a body of Indian opinion within the country as well as outside according to which non-violence is an ideal abstraction incapable of realisation, and that the only way in which Swaraj can ever be attained is by the application of force and violence. I do not for a moment question the sacrifice and patriotism of those who hold this view. I know that some of them have suffered for the cause which they believe to be true. But may I be permitted to point out that apart from any question of principle, history has proved over and over again the utter futility of revolutions brought about by force and violence. I am one of those who hold to non-violence on principle. But let us consider the question of expediency. Is it possible to attain Swaraj by violent means? The answer which history gives is an emphatic "No". Take all the formidable revolutions of the world.

THE FRENCH REVOLUTION

The history of the French Revolution is the history of a struggle at the first instance between the Crown and the nobility on one side and the Representative Assemblies with armed Paris on the other. Both took to violence, one to the bayonet and the other to the pike. The pike succeeded because the bayonet was held with uncertain hands. And then, as is usual after the victory gained with violence, the popular party was sharply divided between two sections—the Girondins and the Jacobins. Again there was an appeal to force. The Girondins asked the provinces to rise in arms, the Jacobins asked Paris to rise in arms. Paris being nearer and stronger, the

Girondins were defeated and sent to the guillotine—the Jacobins seized the power. But it did not take them many months to fall out among themselves. First Robespierre and Danton sent Hebert and Chanmette to the guillotine, then Robespierre sent Danton to the guillotine. Robespierre in his turn was guillotined by Collot, Billand and Tallien. These men again were banished by others to the far-off South America. If there was a slight difference of views between the Girondins and the Jacobins there was practically none between the different sections of the Jacobins. The whole question was which of the various sections was to rule France. Force gave way to stronger force and at last under Napoleon, France experienced a despotism similar to if not worse than the despotism of Louis XIV. As regards liberty there was not more liberty in France under the terrible Committee of Public Safety, and Napoleon than under Louis XIV or Louis XV. The law of Prairial was certainly much worse than Lettres de Cachet. And the people—? On the Pont au Change, on the Place de Greve, in long sheds, Mercier, at the end of the Revolution, saw working men at their repast. One's allotment of daily bread had sunk to an ounce and a half. "Plates containing each three grilled herrings, sprinkled with shorn onions, wetted with a little vinegar; to this add some morsel of boiled prunes, and lentils swimming in a clear sauce; at these frogal tables I have seen them ranged by the hundred; consuming, without bread, their scant messes, far too moderate for the keenness of their appetite, and the extent of their stomach." "Seine water," remarks Carlyle grimly—"rushing plenteous by, will supply the deficiency." One cannot forget the exclamation of Carlyle in this connection:

"O Man of Toil! Thy struggling and thy daring, these six long years of insurrection and tribulation, thou hast profited nothing by it, then? Thou consumest thy herring and water, in the blessed gold-red of evening. O why was the Earth so beautiful, becrimsoned with dawn and twilight, if man's dealings with man were to make it a vale of scarcity, of tears, not even soft tears? Destroying of Bastilles, discomfiting of Brunswicks, fronting of Principalities and Powers, of Earth and Tophet, all that thou hast dared and endured,—it was for a Republic of the Saloons? Aristocracy of Feudal Parchment has passed away with a mighty rushing; and now, by a natural course, we arrive at Aristocracy of the Moneybag. It is the course through which all European Societies are, at this hour, travelling. Apparently a still baser sort of Aristocracy? An infinitely baser the basest yet known."

Even to-day France is plodding her weary way towards Swaraj.

REVOLUTIONS IN ENGLAND

The history of England proves the same truth. The revolution of the Barons in 1215 took away or purported to take away the power from the King but the power fell into the hands of the aristocracy, and democracy did not share in the triumph of the Barons. Thus the great Charter, as a great historian has observed, was thus not a Charter of Liberty but of liberties. The revolution in the reign of Charles I. produced a new dictator who suppressed freedom. The work which the Long Parliament began was interrupted by the Revolution which followed the execution of the King, and it required another Revolution, this time a bloodless Revolution, to complete the work. I deny that the work is yet complete. The continual class war and the obvious economic injustice do not proclaim that freedom which England claimed for herself. I maintain that no people has yet succeeded in winning freedom by force and violence. The truth is that love of power is a formidable factor to be reckoned with, and those who secure that power by violence will retain that power by violence. The use of violence degenerates them who use it and it is not easy for them, having seized the power, to surrender it. And they find it easier to carry on the work of their predecessor, retaining their power in their own hands. Non-violence does not carry with it that degeneration which is inherent in the use of violence.

REVOLUTIONS IN ITALY AND RUSSIA

The Revolutions in Italy and Russia illustrate the same principle. The Italian Revolution inspired by Mazzini and worked out by Garibaldi and Cavour, did not result in the attainment of Swaraj. The freedom of Italy is yet in the making, and the men and women of Italy are to-day looking forward to another revolution. If it results in a war of violence it will again defeat its purpose, but only to allow Freedom and Non-violence to triumph in the end.

The recent revolution in Russia is a very interesting study. The shape which it has now assumed is due to the attempt to force Marxian doctrines and dogmas on the unwilling genius of Russia. Violence will again fail. If I have read the situation accurately I expect a counter-revolution. The soul of Russia must struggle to free herself from the socialism of Carl Marx. It may be an independent movement or it may be that the present movement contains within itself the power of working out that freedom. In the meantime the fate of Russia is trembling in the balance.

NON-VIOLENT NON-CO-OPERATION: THE ONLY METHOD

I believe in revolutions, but I repeat, violence defeats freedom. The revolution of non-violence is slower but surer. Step by step the soul of the nation emerges and step by step the nation marches on in the path of Swaraj. The only method by which Freedom can be attained in India at any rate, is the method of non-violent non-co-operation. Those who believe this method to be impracticable would do well to ponder over the Akali movement. When I saw the injuries of the wounded at Amritsar and heard from their lips that not one of them had even wished to meet violence by violence, in spite of such grave provocation, I said to myself, "here was the triumph of non-violence."

Non-violence is not an idle dream. It was not in vain that Mahatma declared, "put up thy sword into the sheath." Let those who are "of the truth" hear his voice as those others heard a mightier voice two thousand years ago.

The attempt of the Indian nation to attain Swaraj by this method was, however, met by severe repression. The time has come for us to estimate our success as well as our failure. So far as repression is concerned, it is easy to answer the question. I have not the least doubt in my mind that the nation has triumphed over the repression which was started and continued to kill the soul of the movement.

SUCCESS OF NON-VIOLENT NON-CO-OPERATION

But the question, which agitates most minds, is as to whether we have succeeded in our work of non-violent non-co-operation. There is, I am sorry to say, a great deal of confusion of thought behind the question. It is assumed that a movement must either succeed or fail, whereas the truth is that human movements, I am speaking of genuine movements, neither altogether succeed nor altogether fail. Every genuine movement proceeds from an ideal, and the ideal is always higher than the achievement. Take the French revolution. Was it a success? Was it a failure? To predicate either would be a gross historical blunder. Was the non-co-operation movement in India a success? Yes, a mighty success when we think of the desire for Swaraj which it has succeeded in awakening throughout the length and breadth of this vast country. It is a great success when we think of the practical result of such awakening, in the money which the nation contributed, in the enrolment of members of the Indian National Congress and in the boycott of foreign cloth. I go further and say that the practical achievement also consists of the loss of prestige suffered by Educational Institutions and the Courts of Law and the Reformed Councils throughout the country. If they are still resorted to, it is because of the weakness of our countrymen. The country has already expressed its strong desire to end these institutions. Yet it must be admitted that from another point of view, when we assess the measure of our success in the spirit of Arithmetic, we are face to face with "the petty done" and "the undone vast." There is much which remains to be accomplished. Non-violence has to be more firmly established. The work of non-co-operation has to be strengthened, and the field of non-co-operation has to be extended. We must be firm but reasonable. The spirit of sacrifice has got to be further strengthened, and we must proceed with the work of destruction and creation more vigorously than before I say to our critics. I admit we have failed in many directions, but will you also not admit our success where we have succeeded?

CHARGE OF CORRUPTING THE YOUTHS

We have been denounced by the Moderates for having corrupted the youth of this country. It has been asserted that we have taught sons to disobey their fathers, the pupils, their teachers and the subjects the Government. We plead guilty to the charge and we rely on every spiritual movement as argument in our support. Christ himself was tried for having corrupted the people, and the answers which he gave in anticipation is as emphatic as it is instructive.

"Think not that I am come to send peace on earth. I come not to send peace, but a sword."

"For I am come to set a man at variance against his father and the daughter-in-law against her mother-in-law."

CHARGE OF HYPOCRISY

It has been said that with love on our lips we have been preaching the Gospel of hatred. Never was such a vile slander uttered. It may be we have failed to love, it may be we lost ourselves some of us in hatred, but that only shows our weakness and imperfectness. Judge us by our ideals, not by what we have achieved. Wherever we have fallen short of our ideal, put it down to our weakness. On behalf of the Indian National Congress I deny the charge of hypocrisy. To those who are anxious to point out our defects, I say with all humility. "My friends, if you are weak, come and join us and make us stronger. If the Leaders are worthless, come and join us to lead, and the leaders will stand aside. If you do not believe in the ideal what is the use of always criticising us in the light of that ideal?" We need no critic to tell us how far we have fallen short of that ideal. Evidence of weakness has met me from every direction which I have looked. But in spite of our defects of human weakness, of human imperfection I feel bold enough to say that our victory is assured and that the Bureaucracy knows that our victory is assured.

HOW TO APPLY THE NON-VIOLENT N. C. O. METHOD

But though the method of non-violent non-co-operation is sure and certain, we have now to consider how best to apply that method to the existing circumstances of the country. I do not agree with those who think that the spirit of the nation is so dead that non-violent non-co-operation is no longer possible. I have given the matter my earnest thought and I desire to make it perfectly clear that there is absolutely no reason for entertaining any feelings of doubt or despair. The outward appearance of the people to-day is somewhat deceptive. They appear to be in a tired condition and a sense of fatigue has partially overcome them. But beneath all this exterior of quietude, the pulse of the nation beats as strongly as before and as hopefully as at the beginning of this movement. We have to consolidate the strength of the nation. We have to devise a plan of work which will stimulate their energy, so that we can accelerate our journey towards Swaraj. I shall place before you one by one the items of work which in my opinion the Indian National Congress should prescribe for the nation.

DECLARATION OF RIGHTS

It should commence its work for the year, by a clearer declaration of rights of the different communities in India under the Swaraj Government. So far as the Hindus and Mahomedans are concerned, there should be a clear and emphatic confirmation of what is known as the Lucknow pact and along with that there should be an emphatic insistence of each others' rights. And each should be prepared to undergo some kind of sacrifice in favour of the other. Let me give an instant to make my meaning clear. Every devout Mussalman objects to any music in front of a mosque and every devout and orthodox Hindu objects to cows being slaughtered. May not the Hindus and Mussalmans of India enter into a solemn pact so that there may not be any music before any mosque and that no cows may he slaughtered? Other instances may be quoted. There should be a scheme of a series of sacrifices to be suffered by each community so that they may advance shoulder to shoulder in the path of Swaraj. As regards the other communities such as Sikhs, Christians and Parsees, the Hindus and Mohamedans who constitute the bulk of the people should be prepared to give them even more than their proportional share in the Swaraj administration, I suggest that the Congress should bring about real agreement between all these communities, by which the rights of every minority should be clearly recognised in order to remove all doubts which may arise and all apprehensions which probably exist. I need hardly add that I include among Christians not only pure Indians but also Anglo-Indians and other people who have chosen to make India their home. Such an agreement as I have indicated was always necessary but such an agreement is specially necessary in view of the work which faces us to-day.

FOREIGN PROPAGANDA

I further think that the policy of exclusiveness which we have been following during the last two years be now abandoned. There is in every country a number of people who are selfless followers of liberty and who desire to see every country free. We can no longer afford to lose their sympathy and co-operation. In my opinion there should be established Congress agencies in America and in every European country. We must keep ourselves in touch with the world's movements and be in constant communication with the lovers of freedom all over the world.

THE GREAT ASIATIC FEDERATION

Even more important than this is the participation of India in the great Asiatic Federation which I see in the course of formation. I have hardly any doubt that the Pan-Islamic movement which was started on a somewhat narrow basis has given way or is about to give way to the great Federation of all Asiatic people. It is the union of the oppressed nationalities of Asia. Is India to remain outside the union? I admit that our freedom must be won by ourselves, but such a bond of friendship and love of sympathy and co-operation between India and the rest of Asia, nay between India and all the liberty-loving people of the world is destined to bring about World Peace. World Peace, to my mind, means the freedom of every nationality and I go further and say that no nation in the face of the earth can be really free when other nations are in bondage. The policy which we have hitherto pursued, was absolutely necessary for the concentration of the work which we took upon ourselves to perform and I agreed to that policy whole-heartedly. The hope of the attainment of Swaraj or a substantial basis of Swaraj in the course of the year made such concentration absolutely necessary. To-day that very work demands broader sympathy and a wider outlook.

DEMANDS FOR PUNJAB WRONGS, KHILAFAT AND SWARAJ

We are on the eve of great changes, and the world-forces are upon us. The victory of Kemal Pasha has broken the bonds of Asia and she is all astir with life. It is Prometheus who spoke within her, and 'her thoughts' are like the many forests of vale through which the might of whirlwind and rain had passed. The stir within every European country for the real freedom of the people has also worked a marvellous transformation in the mentality of subject races. That which was more or less a matter of Ideal has now come within the range of practical politics. The Indian nation has found out its bearings. At such a time as this it is necessary for us to reconsider and to restate our demands. Our demands regarding the Punjab wrongs have got to be restated because many of them have already been realised. Our demands regarding Khilafat have got to be reconsidered, because some of them have already been worked out and we hope that before Lausanne Commission has finished their work very little of it will remain unrealised. Our demand for Swaraj must now be presented in a more practical shape. The Congress should frame a clear scheme of what we mean by a system of government which may serve as a real foundation for Swaraj. Hitherto, we have not defined any such system of Government. We have not done so advisedly as it was on the psychological aspect of Swaraj that we concentrated our attention. But circumstances to-day have changed. The desire is making us impatient. It is therefore the duty of the Congress to place before the Country a clear scheme of the system of Government which we demand. Swaraj, as I have said, is indefinable and is not to be confused with any particular system of Government. Yet the national mind must express itself, and although the full outward expression of Swaraj covers the whole life history of a nation, the formulation of such a demand cannot be any further delayed.

SCHEME OF A GOVERNMENT

It is hardly within the provincc of this address to deal with any detail scheme of any such Government. I cannot, however, allow this opportunity to pass without giving you an expression of my opinion as to the character of that system of Government. No system of Government which is not for the people and by the people can even be regarded as the true foundation of Swaraj. I am firmly convinced that a parliamentary Government is not a government by the people and for the people. Many of us believe that the middle class must win Swaraj for the masses. I do not believe in the possibility of any class movement being ever converted into a movement for Swaraj. If to-day the British Parliament grants Provincial autonomy in the provinces with responsibility in the Central Government, I for one, will protest against, because that will inevitably lead to the concentration of the power in the hands of the middle class. I do not believe that the middle class will then part with their power. How will it profit India, if in place of the White Bureaucracy that now rules over her, there is substituted an Indian Bureaucracy of the middle classes. Bureaucracy is Bureaucracy and I believe that the very idea of Swaraj is inconsistent with the existence of a Bureaucracy. My ideal of Swaraj will never be satisfied unless the people co-operate with us in its attainment. Any other attempt will inevitably lead to what European Socialists call the "Bourgeoise" Government. In France and in other European countries it is the middle class who fought the battle of freedom and the result is that power is still in the hands of this class. Having usurped the power they are unwilling to face with it. If to-day the whole Europe is engaged in a battle of real freedom it is because the nations of Europe are gathering their strength to wrest this power from the hands of the middle classes. I desire to avoid repetition of that chapter of European history. It is for India to show the light to the world, Swaraj by Non-violence and Swaraj by the people.

To me the organisation of village life and the practical autonomy of small local centres are more important than either provincial autonomy or central responsibility; and if the choice lay between the two, I would unhesitatingly accept the autonomy of the local centres. I must not be understood as implying that the village centres will he disconnected units. They must be held together by a system of co-operation and integration. For the present, there must be power in the hands of the provincial and the Indian Government; but the ideal should be accepted once for all, that the proper function of the central authority, whether in the provincial or in the Indian Government is to advise, having a residuary power of control only in case of need and to be exercised under proper safeguard. I maintain that real Swaraj can only be attained by vesting the power of Government in these local centres, and I suggest that the Congress should appoint a Committee to draw up a scheme of Government which would be acceptable to the Nation.

The most advanced thought of Europe is turning from the false individualism on which European culture and institutions are based to what I know to be the ideal of the ancient village organisation of India. According to this thought modern democracy of the ballot box and large crowds has failed, but real democracy has not yet been tried. What is the real democracy of modern European thought?

The foundation of real democracy must be laid in small centres—not gradual decentralisation which implies a previous centralisation—but a gradual integration of the practically autonomous small centres into one living harmonious whole. What is wanted is a human state, not a mechanical contrivance. We want the growth of institutions and organisations which are really dynamic in their nature and not the mere static stability of a centralised state.

This strain of European thought found some expression in the philosophy of Hegel according to whom "human institutions belong to the region not of inert externality, but of mind and purpose and are therefore dynamic and self-developing."

Modern European thought has made it clear that from the individual to the "unified state," it is one continuous process of real and natural growth. Sovereignity (Swaraj) is a relative notion. "The individual is sovereign over himself"—attains his Swaraj "in so far as he can develop control and unify his manifold nature." From the individual we come to the integrated neighbourhood which is the real foundation of the unified State, which again in its turn gives us the true ideal of the world-state. This integrated neighbourhood is a great deal more than the mere physical contiguity of the people who live in the neighbourhood area. It requires the coalition of what has been called "neighbourhood consciousness." In other words, the question is "how can the force generated by the neighbourhood life become part of our whole critic and national life?" It is this question which now democracy takes upon itself to solve.

The process prescribed is the generation of the collective will. The democracy which obtains to-day rests on an attempt of securing a common will by a process of addition. This really means a war of wills, the issue being left to be decided by a mere superiority of numbers. New democracy discountenances this process of addition, and insists on the discovery of detailed means and methods by which the different wills of a neighbourhood entity may grow into one common collective will. This process is not a process addition but of integration and the consciousness of the neighbourhood thus awakened must express the common collective will of that neighbourhood entity. The collective will of several neighbourhood centres, must by a similar process of integration be allowed to evolve the Common collective will of the whole nation. It is only thus, by a similar process of integration that any league of nations may be real and the vision of a world state may be realized. The whole of this philosophy is based on the idea of the evolution of the individual. The idea is to "release the powers of the individual." Ordinary notions of state have little to do with true individualism, (*i. e.*) with the individual as consciously responsible for the life from which he draws his breath and to which he contributes his all. According to this school of thought 'Representative government, party organisation, majority rule, with all their excrescences in their stead must appear the organisation of non-partisan groups for the begetting, the bringing into being of common ideas, a common purpose and the collective will.' This means the true development and extension of the individual self. The institutions that exist to-day have made machines of men. No Government will be successful, no true Government is possible which does not rest on the individual. "Up to the present moment," says the gifted authoress of the New State, "we have never seen the individual yet. The search for him has been the whole long striving of our Anglo-Saxon history. We sought to improve the method of representation and failed to find him. We sought to reach him by extending the suffrage to every man and then to every woman and yet he eludes us. Direct Government now seeks the individual." In another place the same writer says; "Thus group organisation releases us from the domination of mere numbers, thus democracy transcends time and space. It can never be understood except as a spiritual force. Majority rule rests on numbers; democracy rests on the well-grounded assumption that society is not a collection of units, but a network of human relations. Democracy is not worked out at the polling booths, it is the bringing forth of a genuine collective will, one to which every single being must contribute the whole of his complex life, as one which every single being must express the whole of it at one point. Thus the essence of democracy is creating. The technique of democracy is group organization." According to this school of thought no living state is possible without the development and the extension of the individual self. The State itself is no static unit. Nor is it an arbitrary creation. "It is a process; a continual self-modification to express its different stages of growth in which each and all must be so flexible that continual change of form is twin fellow of continual growth." This can only be realised when there is a clear perception that individuals and groups and the nation stand in no antithesis. The integration of all these into one conscious whole means and must necessarily mean the integration of the wills of individuals into the common and collective will of the entire nation.

The general trend of European thought has not accepted the ideal of this new democracy. But the present problems which are agitating Europe seem to offer no other solution. I have very little doubt that this ideal which appears to many practical politicians as impracticable will be accepted as the real ideal at no distant future. "There is little yet," I again quote from the same author, "that is practical in practical politics."

The fact is that all the progressive movements in Europe have suffered because of the want of a really spiritual basis and it is refreshing to find that this writer has seized upon it. So to those who think that the neighbourhood group is puny to serve as a real foundation of self-Government, she says, "is our daily life profane and only so far as we rise out of it do we approach the sacred life? Then no wonder politics are what they have become. But this is not the creed of men to-day; we believe in the sacredness of life; we believe that divinity is for ever incarnating in humanity, and so we believe in Humanity and the common daily life of all men."

There is thus a great deal of correspondence between this view of life and the view which I have been endeavouring to place before my countrymen for the last 15 years. For the truth of all truths, is that the outer Leela of God reveals itself in history. Individual Society, Nation, and Humanity are the different aspects of that very Leela and no scheme of self-Government which is practically true and which is really practical can be based on any other philosophy of life. It is the realisation of this truth which is the supreme necessity of the hour. This is the soul of Indian thought, and this is the ideal towards which the recent thought of Europe is slowly, but surely, advancing.

To frame such a scheme of Government regard must therefore be had:—

1. To the formation of local centres more or less on the lines of the ancient village system of India.

2. The growth of larger and larger groups out of the integration of these village centres.

3. The unifying state should be the result of minor growth.

4. The village centres and the larger groups must be practically autonomous.

5. The residuary power of control must remain in the Central Government, but the exercise of such power should be exceptional and for that purpose proper safeguards should be provided, so that the practical autonomy of the local centres may be maintained and at the same time the growth of the Central Government into a really unifying state may be possible. The ordinary work of such Central Government should bc mainly advisory.

As a necessary corollary to what I have ventured to suggest as the form of Government which we should accept, I think that the work of organising these local centres should be forthwith commenced. The modern sub-divisions or even smaller units may be conveniently taken as the local centres, and larger centres may be conveniently formed. Once we have our local areas—"the neighbourhood group"—we should foster the habit of corporate thinking, and leave all local problems to be worked out by them. There is no reason why we should not start the Government by these local centres to-day. They would depend for their authority on the voluntary co-operation of the people, and voluntary co-operation is much better than the compulsory co-operation which is at the bottom of the Bureaucratic rule in India. This is not the place to elaborate the scheme which I have in mind; but I think that it is essentially necessary to appoint a Committee with power, not only to draw up a scheme of Government but to suggest means by which the scheme can be put in operation at once.

BOYCOTT OF COUNCILS

The next item of work to which I desire to refer is the Boycott of Councils. Unhappily the question has become part of the controversy of Change or No change. To my mind the whole controversy proceeds on a somewhat erroneous assumption. The question is not so much as to whether there should be a change in the programme of the work; the real question is, whether it is not necessary now to change the direction of our activities in certain respects for the success of the very movement which we hold so dear. Let me illustrate what I mean. Take the Bardoli Resolution. In the matter of boycott of schools and colleges the Bardoli Resolution alters the direction of our activity, which does not in any way involve the abandonment of the boycott. During the Swaraj year the idea was to bring the students out of Government schools and colleges, and if National schools were started they were regarded as concessions to the "weakness" of those students. The idea was, to quote the words of Mahatma Gandhi, "political" and not "educational." Under the Bardoli Resolution, however, it is the establishment of schools and colleges which must be the main activity of national education. The idea is "educational" and if it still be the desire of the Congress to bring students out of Government schools and colleges, it is by offering them educational advantages. Here the boycott of schools and colleges is still upheld, but the direction of our activities is changed. In fact, such changes must occur in every revolution, violent or non-violent, as it is only by such changes that the ideal is truly served.

In the next place, we must keep in view the fact that according to the unanimous opinion of the members of the Enquiry Committee, Civil Disobedience on a large scale is out of question because the people are not prepared for it.

I confess that I am not in favour of the restrictions which have been put upon the practical adoption of any system of civil disobedience, and in my opinion, the Congress should abolish those restrictions. I have not yet been able to understand why to enable a people to civilly disobey particular laws, it should be necessary that at least 80 per cent. of them should be clad in pure "Khadi". I am not much in favour of general Mass Civil Disobedience. To my mind, the idea is impracticable. But the disobedience of particular laws which are eminently unlawful, laws which are the creatures of "Law and Order," laws which are like an outrage on humanity and an insult to God ... disobedience of such laws is within the range of practical politics, and, in my opinion, every attempt should be made to offer disobedience to such laws. It is only by standing on truth that the cause of Swaraj may prevail. When we submit to such laws, we abandon the plank of truth. What hope is there for a nation so dead to the sense of truth as not to rebel against lawless laws, against regulations which insult their national being and hamper their national development?

I am of opinion that the question of the boycott of Councils which is agitating the country so much must be considered and decided in the light of the circumstances I have just mentioned. There is no opposition in idea between such civil disobedience as I have mentioned and the entry into the Councils for the purpose and with the avowed object of either ending or mending them. I am not against the boycott of Councils. I am simply of opinion that the system of the Reformed Councils with their steel frame of the Indian Civil Service covered over by a dyarchy of deadlocks and departments is absolutely unsuitable to the nature and genius of the Indian nation. It is an attempt of the British Parliament to force a foreign system upon the Indian people. India has unhesitatingly refused to recognise this foreign system as real foundation for Swaraj. With me, as I have often said, it is not a question of more or less; I am always prepared to sacrifice much for a real basis of Swaraj, nor do I attach any importance to the question as to whether the attainment of full and complete independence will be a matter of 7 years or 10 years or 20 years. A few years is nothing in the life history of a nation. But I maintain India cannot accept a system such as this as a foundation of Swaraj. These Councils must therefore be either mended or ended. Hitherto we have been boycotting the Councils from outside. We have succeeded in doing much. The prestige of the councils is diminished and the country knows that the people who adorn those chambers are not the true representatives of the people. But though we have succeeded in doing much, these Councils are still there. It shall be the duty of the Congress to boycott the councils more effectively from within. Reformed councils are really a mask which the Bureaucracy has put on. I conceive it to be our clear duty to tear this mask from off their face. The very idea of boycott implies, to my mind, something more than mere withdrawal. The boycott of foreign goods means that such steps must be taken that these councils may not be there to impede the progress of Swaraj. The only successful boycott of these councils is either to mend them in a manner suitable to the attainment of Swaraj or to end them completely. That is the way in which I advise the nation to boycott the councils.

A great deal of discussion has taken place in the country as to whether the boycott of councils in the sense in which I mean it is within the principle of non-violent non-co-operation. I am emphatically of opinion that it does not offend against any principle of non-co-operation which has been adopted and applied by the Indian National Congress. I am not dealing with the logical, or philosophical abstractions. I am only dealing with that which the Congress has adopted and called non-co-operation. In the first place, may I point out that we have not up to now non-co-operated with the Bureaucracy? We have been merely preparing the people of this country to offer non-co-operation. Let me quote the Nagpur Resolution on non-co-operation in support of my proposition. I am quoting only the portions which are relevant to this point.

Whereas in the opinion of the Congress the existing Government of India has forfeited the confidence of the country, and, whereas the people of India are now determined to establish Swaraj ... now this Congress ... declares that the entire or any part or parts of the scheme of non-violent non-co-operation with the renunciation of voluntary association with the present Government at one end and the refusal to pay taxes at the other, should be put into force at a time to be determined by either the Indian National Congress, or the All-India Congress Committee and that "in the meanwhile to prepare the country for it, effective steps should continue to be taken in that behalf."

Then follows the effective steps such as, national education, boycott of law courts, boycott of foreign goods, etc., which must be taken "in the meanwhile." It is clear therefore that the Congress has not yet advocated the application of non-co-operation but has merely recommended certain steps to be taken so that at some time or other to be determined by the Congress, the Indian Nation may offer non-co-operation. In the second place, let us judge of the character of this principle not by thinking of any logical idea or philosophical abstraction but by gathering principle from the work and the activity which the Congress has enjoined. When I survey the work it is clear to my mind that the Congress was engaged in a two-fold activity. In everything that the Congress has commanded there is an aspect of destruction as there is an aspect of creation. The boycott of Lawyers and Law Courts means the destruction of existing legal institutions; and the formation of Panchayats means the creation of agencies through which justice may be administered. The boycott of schools and colleges means the destruction of the department of Education; and the establishment of National schools and colleges means the creation of educational institutions for the Youth of India. The boycott of foreign goods followed as it was by the burning of foreign goods covering into the country. But, on the other hand, the spinning wheel and looms means creative activity in supplying the people with indigenous cloth. Judged by this principle what is wrong about the desire either to convert the Councils into institutions which may lead us to Swaraj, or to destroy them altogether? The same twofold aspect of creation and destruction is to be found in the boycott of Councils in the way I want them to be boycotted.

It has also been suggested that it offends against the morality and spirituality of this movement. Let us take the two points separately. As regards morality apart from the ethics of Non-co-operation, it has been urged that entering the Councils for the purpose of ending the Councils is unfair and dishonest. The argument implies that the Reformed Councils belong entirely to the Bureaucracy, and the idea is that we should not enter into other peoples' property with a view to injure it. To my mind, the argument is based on a misconception of facts. Inadequate as the Reforms undoubtedly are, I do not for a moment admit that the Reform Act was a gift of the British Parliament. It was, to quote the words of Mahatma Gandhi, "a concession to popular agitation." The fact is that it is the resultant of two contending forces, the desire of the people for freedom and the desire of the Bureaucracy to oppose such a desire. The result is that it has travelled along lines neither entirely popular nor entirely bureaucratic. The people of India do not like these Reforms, but let us not forget that the Bureaucracy does not like them either because it is the result of two contending forces pulling in different directions or the Reforms have assumed a tortured state. But so far as the rights recognised are concerned, they are our rights—our property, and there is nothing immoral or unfair or dishonest in making use of the rights which the people have extorted from the British Parliament. If the fulfilment of the very forces which have succeeded in securing the Reforms require that the Councils should either be mended or ended, if the struggle for freedom compels the adoption of either course, what possible charge of immorality can be levelled against it? I admit if we had proposed to enter the Councils stealthily with the avowed object of co-operation keeping within our hearts the desire to break the Councils, such a course would undoubtedly have been dishonest. European diplomacy, let us hope, has been abolished by Indian National Congress under the leadership of Mahatma Gandhi. If we play now, we play with all our cards on the table.

But some people say that it is immoral from the point of view of non-co-operation, because it involves an idea of destruction. The work of non-co-operation according to these,—I have the highest reverence for them,—is only to build our national life ignoring altogether the existence of the Bureaucracy. It may be an honest ideal, and, logically speaking, it may be the inner meaning of non-co-operation. But the non-co-operation which the Congress has followed is not so logical and I claim that if the principle of non-co-operation is to be advanced as a test of my programme, let it be the same principle which the Congress has accepted, adopted and applied. As I have already said, that principle countenance destruction as well as creation. As a matter of fact circumstanced as we are with Bureaucracy to the right and the Bureaucracy to the left Bureaucracy all around us, it is impossible to create without destroying: nor must it be forgotten that if we break, it is only that we may build.

It has also been suggested that the very entry into the Council is inconsistent with the ideal of non-co-operation. I confess I do not understand the argument. Supposing the Congress had sanctioned an armed insurrection could it be argued that entry into the fort of the Bureaucracy is inconsistent with the principle of non-co-operation? Surely the charge of inconsistency must depend on the object of the entry. An advancing army does not co-operate with the enemy when it marches into the enemy's territory. Co-operation must therefore depend on the object with which such entry is made. The argument if analysed comes to this, that whenever the phrase entry into Councils is used it calls up the association of co-operation, and then the mere idea of this entry is proclaimed to be inconsistent with non-co-operation. But this is the familiar logical fallacy of our terms. Entry into the Councils to co-operate with the Government and entry into the Councils to non-co-operate with the Government are two terms and two different propositions. The former is inconsistent with the idea of non-co-operation, the latter is absolutely consistent with that very idea.

Next let us understand the opposition from the point of view of the spirituality of our movement. The question of spirituality is not to be confused with the dictates of any particular religion. I am not aware of the injunctions of any religion against entering the Councils with a view either to mend them or end them. I have heard from many Mahomedans that the Koran lays down no such injunction. Other Mahomedan friends have told me that there may be some difficulty on that ground, but that is a matter with regard to which I am not competent to speak. The Khilafat must answer that question with such assistance as they may obtain from the Ulemas. It is needless to point out that should the Ulemas come to the conclusion that under the present circumstances it would be an offence against their religion to enter the Councils, the Congress should unhesitatingly accept their decision because no work in this country towards the attainment of Swaraj is possible without the hearty co-operation of both Hindus and Mussalmans. But I am dealing with that spirituality which does not affect any particular creed or any particular religion. Judged from the standpoint of such spirituality what objection there can be in removing from our path by all legitimate means any obstacle to the attainment of Swaraj? We burned foreign cloth without a scruple, and the spirituality of the movement did not receive a shock when we burned them. It is as well to start with a clear conception as to what that spiritually is. Apart from any creedal or doctrinal injunction and apart from any question of morality, the basis of spirituality must be the attainment of freedom and of Swaraj. What is the duty which every human being owes not only to his race, not only to his nation, not only to humanity but also to his God? It is the right to fulfil oneself. It is the duty of living in the light of God. Shortly after my release from imprisonment I said in a public speech that all our national activities should be based on truth. Ever since that day questions and conundrums have been put to me. I have been asked to define what is truth. It has also been suggested that because I dare not tell the truth that I took refuge under the general expression. I still insist that our national activities must be based on truth. I repeat that I do not believe in politics, or in making water-tight compartments of our national life which is an indivisible organic whole. I repeat that as you cannot define life, you cannot define truth. The test of Truth is not logical definition. The test of Truth lies in its all-compelling force, in making itself felt. You know truth when you have felt it. God cannot be defined, nor can truth because truth is the revelation of God. Two thousand years ago, a jesting judge asked the same question of the Son of God. He made no answer by word of mouth; but he sacrificed himself and Truth was revealed. When I speak of spirituality I speak of the same truth. I look upon history as the revelation of God. I look upon human individual personality, nationality and humanity, each contributing to the life of the other as the revelation of God to man. I look upon the attainment of freedom and Swaraj the only way of fulfilling oneself as individuals, as nations. I look upon all national activities as the real foundation of the service of that greater humanity which again is the revelation of God to man. The Son of God brought to the world not peace but a sword—not the peace of death and immortality and corruption but the "separating sword" of Truth. We have to fight against all corruptions and all immorality. It is only thus that freedom can be attained. Whatever obstacles there may be in the path of Swaraj either of the individual or of the nation, or humanity at large, these obstacles must be removed by the individual if he desires his freedom by the nation, if that nation desires to ruin itself by all the nations of the world if the cause of humanity is to prosper. That being the spirituality of the movement as I understand it I am prepared to put away all obstacles that lie between the Indian nation and the attainment of its freedom, not stealthily but openly, reverently in the name of truth and God. Judged from this ideal of spirituality the entry into the Councils for the purpose I have stated is necessary to advance the cause of truth. Everything in connection with the controversy must be judged by that standard.

At present the question before the country put by those members of the Civil Disobedience Enquiry Committee who are in favour of the Council Entry is simply that the members of the Congress should stand as candidates. It is unnecessary therefore to go into other questions raised, such as in the matter of taking oath, the probability or otherwise of securing a majority and so on. With regard to the question of oath all that I need say at present is this, that apart from the dictates of any particular religion which I do not propose to deal with, the question does not present any difficulty at all. The oath is a constitutional one. The king stands for the constitution. Great changes in the constitution have taken place in England under that very oath. Now what is the oath? It binds those who take it,—first not to make any use of powers which are not allowed by the Reforms Act; secondly to discharge their duties faithfully. So far as the first point is concerned, there is nothing in my suggestion which militates against it. So far as the second point is concerned, I am aware that a forced interpretation has been sought to be put upon it, namely, that a member taking the oath is bound to discharge his duties faithfully to the Bureaucracy. All that I need say is, that there is no constitutional authority of any kind to justify that interpretation. To my mind the words mean a faithful discharge of a member's duties to his constituency by the exercise of powers recognised under the Reforms Act. I do not therefore understand what possible objection there may be to take the Oath. But there again the question does not arise at present.

Various other questions have been asked as to whether it is possible to secure a majority and as to what we should do, supposing we are in a majority. I think it possible that having regard to the present circumstances of the country, the Non-co-operators are likely to get the majority. I am aware of the difficulty of the franchise. I am aware of the rules which prevent many of us from entering the Councils; but making every allowances for all these difficulties, I believe that we shall be in the majority. But here also the question doesn't arise till we meet in the Congress of 1923 when the matter may be discussed not on suppositions but on actualities.

As regards the question as to what we should do if we have the majority the answer is clear. We should begin our proceedings by a solemn declaration of the existence of our inherent right, and by formal demand for a constitution which would recognise and conserve those rights and give effect to our claims for the particular system of Government which we may choose for ourselves. If our demands are accepted, then the fight is over. But, as I have often said, if it is conceded that we are entitled to have that form of Government which we may choose for ourselves, and the real beginning is made with that particular form of Government in view, then it matters nothing to me whether the complete surrender of power is made up to-day, or in five years or even in twenty years. If, however, our demand is not given effect to, we must non-co-operate with the Bureaucracy by opposing each and every work of the Council. We must disallow the entire Budget. We must move the adjournment of the House on every possible occasion and defeat every Bill that may be introduced. In fact we must so proceed that the Council will refuse to do any work unless and until our demands are satisfied. I am aware of the large powers of certification which Governors can exercise under the Reform Act. But Government by certification is just as impossible as Government by veto. Such procedure may be adopted on a few occasions. The time must soon come when the Bureaucracy must yield or withdraw the Reforms Act. In either case it is a distinct triumph for the nation, and either course if adopted by the Bureaucracy will bring us nearer to the realisation of our ideal.

Another question is often asked, suppose we end these Reformed Councils,—what then? Could not the same question be asked with regard to every step the Congress has hitherto undertaken in the way of breaking, of destroying institutions. If we had succeeded in destroying the Educational Department, might not somebody ask—what then? If we had succeeded in destroying the legal institutions, might not the question be put with equal relevance? The fact is destruction itself will never bring us Swaraj. The fact further is that no construction is possible without destruction. We must not forget that it is not this activity or that activity by itself that can bring Swaraj. It is the totality of our national activity in the way of destruction and in the way of creation, that will bring Swaraj. If we succeeded in demolishing these Reformed Councils you will find the whole nation astir with life. Let them put other obstacles in our way; we shall remove them with added strength and greater vitality.

It has also been suggested that the Bureaucracy will never allow the Non-co-operators to enter the Councils, they will alter the rules to prevent such entry. I cannot conceive of anything better calculated to strengthen the cause of Non-co-operation than this. If any such rule is framed I should welcome it and again change the direction of our activity. The infant nation in India requires constant struggle for its growth and development. We must not forget that a great non-violent revolution is on the land, and we shall change the direction of our activities as often as circumstances require it. To-day the Councils are open and we must attack them,—to-morrow if the Councils are closed, we must be prepared to deal with the contingency when it arises. What do we do when it pours with rain? We turn our umbrella in the direction from which the water comes. It is in the same way that we must turn the direction of our activities whenever the fulfilment of our national life demands it.

The work of the Councils for the last two years has made it necessary for non-co-operators to enter the Councils. The Bureaucracy has received added strength from these Reformed Councils, and those who have entered the Councils, speaking generally, have practically helped the cause of Bureaucracy. What is most necessary to consider is the fact that taxation has increased by leaps and bounds. The expenditure of the Government of India has grown enormously since the pre-war year 1913-14. In that year the total expenditure of the Government of India amounted to 79 crores and 37 lakhs; in 1919-20, it rose to 138 crores, and in 1920-21, the first year of the reformed system of administration, it stood at 149 crores. The expenses of the current year are likely to be even higher. To meet the successive increases in expenditure, additional taxation was levied in 1916-17, 1917-18, 1919-20, 1921-22 and 1922-23. We may prepare ourselves for proposals for further additional taxation in the ensuing year. In spite of the levy of additional taxation, seven out of the last nine years have been years of deficit.

The increase in military expenditure is chiefly responsible for the present financial situation. In 1913-14, the expenses of this department amounted to about 31½ crores, in 1919-20, after the conclusion of the war they mounted up to 87 crores, and in 1920-21 they stood at 88 crores. As Sir Visveswaraya remarks the expenses under the head "Civil Administration" also have shown a perpetual tendency to increase. As a part and parcel of the Reform Scheme, the emoluments of the members of the Indian Civil Service, the Indian Educational Service, the Indian Medical Service and of all the other services recruited in England have been enormously increased; and to maintain some kind of fairness the salaries of the subordinate services which are manned by Indians have also been increased.

The financial situation in the provinces is not much better. Under the financial arrangements of the Reform Scheme, the provinces of India, taken together, secured an accession to their resources of about 11 crores of Rupees. Besides, the provinces had between them in 1920-21 a total accumulated balance of 21 crores and 68 lakhs. But so great has been the increase in provincial expenditure during the last two years that even those provinces which had hoped to realise large surpluses are now on the verge of bankruptcy. In the first year of the reform era, most of the provinces were faced with deficits and were just able to tide over their financial difficulties by drawing upon their balances. But in the current year, the financial situation in many of the provinces has become worse. The Burma budget shows a deficit of 1 crore and 90 lakhs, the Punjab, 1 crore and 30 lakhs, Bihar and Orissa, 51 lakhs, Madras, 41 lakhs, the United Provinces, 27 lakhs and the Central Provinces 37 lakhs. The deficit of the Madras

Government would have been much higher had it not taken steps to increase its revenues by Rs. 77½ lakhs from fresh taxation. The Bengal statement shows an estimated surplus owing to the remission of the Provincial contribution to the Central Government and expected receipts from fresh taxation amounting to 1 crore and 40 lakhs. But it is very doubtful if the expectation will be realised, and early next year, further fresh taxes are likely to be imposed. Assam has budgeted for a deficit of 14½ lakhs after the imposition of additional taxation. Proposals for further taxation are under consideration in the Punjab, Bihar and Orissa, the Central Provinces and Assam. In the United Provinces the proposals brought forward by the Government were rejected by the Legislative Council.

I warn my countrymen against the policy of allowing these Reformed Councils to work their wicked will. There will undoubtedly be a further increase of taxation and there is an apprehension in my mind, I desire to express it with all the emphasis that I can command, that if we allow this policy of drift to continue the result will be that we shall lose the people who are with us to-day. Let us break the Councils if the Bureaucracy does not concede to the demands of the people. If there is fresh taxation as it is bound to be let the responsibility be on the Bureaucracy. Then you and I and the people will jointly fight the powers that be.

LABOUR ORGANISATION

I am further of opinion that the Congress should take up the work of Labour and Peasant organisation. With regard to labour there is a resolution of the Nagpur Congress, but I am sorry to say that it has not been acted upon. There is an apprehension in the minds of some non-co-operators that the cause of non-co-operation will suffer if we exploit Labour for Congress purposes. I confess again I do not understand the argument. The word "exploitation" has got an ugly association, and the argument assumes that Labour and Peasants are not with us in this struggle of Swaraj. I deny the assumption. My experience has convinced me that labour and the Peasantry of India to-day are, if anything, more eager to attain Swaraj than the so called middle and educated classes. If we are "exploiting" boys of tender years and students of colleges, if we are exploiting the women of India, if we are exploiting the whole of the middle classes irrespective of their creed and caste and occupation, may I ask what justification is there for leaving out Labourers and the Peasants? I suppose the answer is that they are welcome to be the members of the Congress Committees but that there should not be a separate organisation of them. But Labour has got a separate interest and they are often oppressed by foreign capitalists and the Peasantry of India is often oppressed by a class of men who are the standard bearers of the Bureaucracy. Is the service of this special interest in any way antagonistic to the service of nationalism? To find bread for the poor, to secure justice to a class of people who are engaged in a particular trade or avocation—how is that work different from the work of attaining Swaraj? Anything which strengthens the national cause, anything which supports the masses of India is surely as much a matter of Swaraj as any other items of work which the Congress has in hand. My advice is that the Congress should lose no time in appointing a Committee, a calm workable Committee to organise labour, and the peasantry of India. We have delayed the matter already too long. If the Congress fails to do its duty, you may expect to find organisations set up in the country by labour and peasants detached from you, dissociated from the cause of Swaraj which will inevitably bring within the arena of a peaceful evolution class struggles and the war of special interests. If the object of the Congress be to avoid that disgraceful issue let us take labour and the peasantry in hand, and let us organise them both from the point of view of their own special interests and also from the point of view of the higher ideal which demands the satisfaction of their special interests and the devotion of such interests to the cause of Swaraj. Here again we have to make use of very selfishness of the labourers and peasants, as we know that the fulfilment of that very selfishness requires its just and proper contribution to the life of the nation.

WORK ALREADY TAKEN UP

I now turn to the work which the Congress has already taken up. I may at once point out that it is not my desire that any work which the Congress has taken up should be surrendered. The change of direction which I advocate and the other practical change which I have mentioned is not by way of surrendering anything that is already on the plank but it is simply by way of addition.

BOYCOTT OF SCHOOLS AND COLLEGES

I am firmly of opinion that the boycott of schools and colleges should be carried on as effectively as before. I defer from the Civil Disobedience Enquiry Committee when they propose the abandonment of the withdrawal of boys from such schools and colleges. The question to my mind is of vital importance. It is on the youth of the country that the cause of Swaraj largely depends—and what chance is there for a nation which willingly, knowingly sends its boys, its young men to schools and colleges to be stamped with the stamps of slavery and foreign culture? I do not desire to enter into the question more minutely. I have expressed my views on the subject so often that I find it unnecessary to repeat them. I, however, agree with the recommendation of the Enquiry Committee that national schools and colleges should also be started.

BOYCOTT OF LAW COURTS AND LAWYERS

With regard to the question of the boycott of lawyers and the legal institutions I agree with the main recommendations of the Committee. Many questions have been raised as to whether the right of defence should be allowed or not and on what occasions, and for what purposes. I have never been in love with formal rules, and I think it impossible to frame rules which will cover all the circumstances which may arise in particular cases. All that I desire to insist on, is the keeping in view of the principle of the boycott of courts.

HINDU-MUSLIM UNITY

With regard to the question of Hindu-Muslim Unity, untouchability and such matters, I agree with the recommendations of the Enquiry Committee. I desire to point out however the true unity of all sections of the Indian nation can only be based on a proper co-operation and the recognition by each section of the rights of the others—that is why I proposed that there should be a compact between different sections, between the different communities of India. We will do little good to the section known as untouchables if we approach them in a spirit of superiority. We must engage them in the work before us, and we must work with them side by side and shoulder to shoulder.

KHADDAR

I now come to the question of khaddar which I regard as one of the most important questions before us. As I have already said, I am opposed to the manufacture of Khaddar on a commercial basis. I said among the other things when I seconded the Bezwada resolution on the 31st of March in 1921 proposed by Mahatma Gandhi:

"Our reason in asking the people to take to Charka was not based upon any desire to enter into any competition with foreign capitalist production either from without or from within. Our idea is to enable the people to understand and fashion for themselves, their economic life and utilise the spare time of their families and opportunities with a view to create more economic goods for themselves and improve their own condition." The idea is to make the people of this country self-reliant and self-contained. This work is difficult but essential and should be carried on with all our strength. I would much rather that few families were self-contained than that factories were started on a large scale. Such factories represent a short-sighted policy, and there is no doubt that though it would satisfy the present need it will create an evil which it would be difficult to eradicate. I am naturally opposed to the creation of a new Manchester in India of which we have had sufficient experience. Let us avoid that possibility, if we can.

It is often stated that Khaddar alone will bring us Swaraj. I ask my countrymen in what way is it possible for khaddar to lead us to Swaraj? It is in one sense only that the statement may be true. We must regard khaddar as the symbol of Swaraj. As the khaddar makes us self-contained with regard to a very large department of our national life, so it is hoped that the inspiration of khaddar will make the whole of our national life self-contained and independent. That is the meaning of the symbol. To my mind such symbol worship requires the spreading out of all non-co-operation activities in every possible direction. It is only thus and only thus that the speedy attainment of Swaraj is possible.

CONCLUSION

It remains to me to deliver to you a last message of hope and confidence. There is no royal road to freedom, and dark and difficult will be the path leading to it. But dauntless is your courage, and firm your resolution; and though there will be reverses, sometimes severe reverses, they will only have the effect of speeding your emancipation from the bondage of a Foreign Government. Do not make the mistake of confusing achievements with success. Achievement as in appearances are often deceptive. I contend that, though we cannot point to a great deal as solid achievement of the movement, the success of it is assured. That success is proclaimed by the bureaucracy in the repeated attempts which were made, and are still being made, to crush the growth of the movement, and to arrest its progress, in the refusal to repeal some of the most obnoxious of the repressive legislation, in the frequent use that has been made of the arbitrary or discretionary authority that is vested in the executive Government and in sending to prison our beloved leader, who offered himself as a sacrifice to the wrath of the Bureaucracy. But though the ultimate success of the movement is assured, I warn you that the issue depends wholly on you and how you conduct yourselves in meeting the forces that are arrayed against you. Christianity rose triumphant when Jesus of Nazareth offered himself as a sacrifice to the excessive worship of law and order by the Scribes and the Pharisees. The forces that are arrayed against you are the forces not only of the bureaucracy but of the modern Scribes and Pharisees whose interest it is to maintain the Bureaucracy in all its pristine glory. Be it yours to offer yourself as sacrifice in the interest of truth and justice, so that your children and your children's children may have the fruit of your sufferings. Be it yours to wage a spiritual warfare so that the victory, when it comes does not debase you, nor tempt you to retain the power of Government in your own hands. But if yours is to be a spiritual warfare, your weapons must be those of the spiritual soldier. Anger is not for you, hatred is not for you, nor for you is pettiness, meanness or falsehood.

For you is the hope of dawn and the confidence of the morning, and for you is the song that was sung by Titan, chained and imprisoned, but the champion of man in the Greek fable:

To Suffer woes with Hope, things infinite;
To forgive wrongs darker than death or night;
To defy power which seems Omnipotent:
To love, and bear, to hope till Hope creates
From its own wreck, the thing it contemplates;
Neither to change, nor falter, nor repent;
This like thy glory, Titan, is to be
Good, Great and joyous, beautiful and free;
This alone Life, Joy, Empire and Victory.
BANDE MATARAM.